[design•*ology*] (NOUN)

FOR WOMEN IN CHARGE

TRUTH AND LIES ABOUT INTERIOR DESIGN

By

Sheryl McLean

Award-winning Architect and Designer

ISBN: 978-1544054711

www.DecoriaDesigns.com

Endorsements and Accolades

"Sheryl made sure she understood my style, she then took it to new, exciting heights, gently guiding me to a fresh, clean look with smooth lines that is so me."

"Sheryl has a great eye for those little details that make the design super special and ensure that the rooms flow together. She managed everything from start to finish so well that I didn't have to do anything but approve the final selections!"

"Sheryl listens carefully to my preferences but encourages me to consider new things that are sometimes a little outside my comfort zone -- wow, I am so glad I listened and followed her advice -- the end result is so much better than I ever could have imagined."

"It always amazes me the way Sheryl draws upon her Architecture and Interior Design background to come up with unique and creative solutions for her clients. Her wealth of knowledge and exciting world travels brings an individualized design sensibility to each project. I'm proud to have her as a colleague."

"Sheryl McLean is the most talented designer I have ever met. Her work is beyond amazing...it is spectacular! Her background as an architect puts her in a class all by herself."

Dedication

This Work is Dedicated to:

My wonderful husband Reggie McLean, family and friends who have always loved and supported me.

Special Thanks to:

Liana Chaouli, Denise Rushing, Carol Cole-Lewis, Chela Sanchez, and my forever Style Sanctuary sisters.

A Gift for You

For your complimentary *Design•ology Checklist:*

How to Hire a Designer That Will Work For YOU, visit

www.designologybook.com

Forward

This is not your ordinary book about interior design. And after all… Sheryl McLean is not your ordinary designer.

I first met Sheryl at a women's business conference. From across the room, we noticed each other. Sheryl is not shy with her opinions and neither am I. Somehow I just knew that Sheryl and I would be working together. We discovered that we each help female CEOs up-level their lives. My medium is wardrobe. Sheryl's is interior design.

We couldn't wait to refer clients to one another and to both up-level our own companies by our association with one another. We were surprised at how similar our philosophies are.

I believe that beauty is one of our birthrights. Every woman deserves to surround herself with beauty in her life, beauty that evokes her joy and reflects her essence. For executive women it is not a luxury, it is a necessity. To embark on such a journey is a process of self-discovery and claiming one's full power.

As women executives, we have a difficult time being vulnerable. I get it. I am the CEO of Image Therapists International. For over 30 years I have helped both men and women executives look and feel magnificent. To up-level your life requires stepping into the unknown, being vulnerable… putting oneself in the care of someone who knows more about that particular art than you do.

And I can say unequivocally that "women in charge" have a tougher road.

Every woman deserves to feel beautiful and to be surrounded by beauty! Every woman deserves to feel magnificent in their own skin, to experience their own beauty, to surround themselves with a beauty that is uniquely their own. What I do with wardrobe, Sheryl McLean does with interior design. She puts the YOU in your home.

I remember Sheryl when she first came into our home—the grace with which she approached us in our own space. I witnessed a beautiful thread of consciousness in her, a sacred thread. It shows in how she holds people, in the way she lets you be and speaks about the space that you live in. We felt held in our own realm with so much dignity, honesty, grace and love--and that is what comes out in her designs. Sheryl literally ministers unto people regarding their homes and their environment. Her graciousness exceeds any situation.

Sheryl teaches you how to surround yourself with design elements that bring you to life, the finer things that make you smile, that evoke joy and renew your spirit, that remind you how strong and uniquely beautiful you are, that speak directly to your soul… even if you don't know where to begin.

Why listen to Sheryl? Well, it's not just that Sheryl is an UCLA-trained architect and international design expert, or that for nearly thirty years she traveled the world with an eye on culture, architecture and design. It's because Sheryl is the kind of woman who knows what is in your closet and will never tell, who listens to your heart without judgment. She helps you create a place that reflects who you are and where you are in life…a space that nurtures you so that you feel amazing.

I trust Sheryl with my life.

Pay attention to what she says. You will not only learn the importance of interior design to up-leveling your life, you will learn how to get there from here.

You deserve it. You've earned it.

--Liana Chaouli, CEO, Image Therapists International

Table of Contents

Introduction: Getting to Wow

d randolph foulds photography

The Female CEO

Some of my clients feel the pressure of always having to be perfect.

These are powerful women. Most are CEOs who have very little spare time and are extremely busy with the many demands placed on them. They are also almost always in control of everything. These women tend to be directive and demand a great deal from those around them. This is not a negative, but it does reflect what their profession is demanding of them. They are on stage, in front of many people, all eyes and ears are listening to them, and judging them most of the time.

Sound familiar?

If you are like most women in top leadership positions, all this comes at a cost. You have spent many years working hard in school and/or on the job in your professional career making sure you were the best at everything. Now, your business dominates most of your time and attention, perhaps keeping you away from your family, your community and your social life. If so, you especially want your home to be a place that truly reflects the accomplishments and dreams you have for your life, surrounded by the beautiful things you desire and for which you have worked so hard.

You need and want to be in an environment where you can be yourself, where you can really enjoy the fruit of your labor. You also want your home to be authentic, not just something you saw in a magazine or on television. You deeply desire a place that truly expresses who you are. If you are like most female CEOs, you need that. You want a quiet space, a place where you can think, where you are not pressured or judged. You long for comfort and warmth. Why? Perhaps it is because you work in an environment where there is very little warmth--where there is a "dog eat dog" attitude--a great deal of competition at all times.

If this is true for you, you definitely do not want any struggle or competition in your own home. You want there to be enjoyment and relaxation. If you have a family, you want quality family time with everyone thriving, happy and enjoying their space. Perhaps you want something that is colorful and bright, not necessarily in terms of the actual colors, but richness within the space. Perhaps you feel that you are on center stage in most arenas of your life, so when you come home, you want the real deal. You want something solid, a place that is truly grounded in the sense of "home."

Make Your Home Yours

Imagine living in a world where your environment was designed especially for you. Imagine your home as the place where you literally experience the same feelings that you have when on vacation--totally relaxed and stress free. So much so, that as you enter your home it wraps itself around you and says, "Welcome home, you are loved, protected and safe. I am going to hold all of the goodness and positive energy that you have in this very special place that is just for you and your family."

Luxury 5-star hotels spend millions of dollars in advertising, marketing and design to convey the sense of 'home away from home'. Isn't it ironic that in many cases the opposite is occurring? Why is it not a reality? If you are in position financially, why is it just a fantasy? Have you put yourself on the back burner--perhaps so far back that the closest connection to your dream is a strange hotel room? I want better for you!

Many powerful, successful people have beautiful houses and yet, they really do not enjoy their homes. Those places may not really be for them because they feel a certain disconnect in their own home! Perhaps they turned the design process over to a professional designer and basically said, "Just create whatever you think is stylish and the best."

I am here to tell you--this is a recipe for disaster. Create the perfect space for whom? If you are not involved, communicating with your designer so that they understand you and what your needs are, then whose personality is going to be expressed in that design? Certainly not yours.

A great designer wants to know: Who is going to be experiencing the space? How do they want to feel in the space? This is important because those occupying the space must and should influence the design. For example, I can create a space where everyone is interacting and having fun, or I can create a more somber and contemplative space where interaction is kept at a minimum. The physical design can influence either of these realities.

If a client of mine says: "I really do not know what to do or what I want, so you just do whatever you think is best." I encourage them to imagine how they want to feel in their space and what elements evoke those feelings. I want them to focus on what would change in their life if they experienced those feelings everyday. How would that benefit them?

Interior design can be a process of self-discovery. If you are a woman in charge and are experiencing the struggle of not having the home environment that you most want, or if you desire a place where you can find an escape from your high-powered, high-pressure work situation, and at the same time be proud to invite others to your home, then this book is for you. In the coming chapters I am going to show you why you need a home that will support and nurture you and what you need to do, so that you can have it.

--Sheryl McLean, Spring 2017

A Design Professional Tells All

d randolph foulds photography

Why Most Female CEOs Struggle With Their Own Homes

A designer is meeting with you to talk about your home. What is going through your head? Chances are all of these thoughts are going through your mind at the same time:

First, What does this have to do with my being happy?

Second, What is expected of me? What if I do not know how to do this?

Third, How much is this going to cost me? Is this going to break the bank?

In addition, as a high-powered executive, you may find yourself needing to provide social entertainment. Perhaps you entertain other executives, those reporting to you, or even clients, in your home. Your dinner parties are not necessarily with friends, but with colleagues. In this sense, your home is about your business, about your brand. This may create a lot of pressure--your colleagues are going to be in your home and it is not perfect. You feel exposed. Some women even feel like a fraud for not walking the talk of excellence they use at work. What are they going to see? What are they going to think or say? The pressure of sharing your home with your colleagues, fearing that you will be judged can cause a lot of anxiety. Especially, when you don't think it's 'perfect'. At times this pressure can feel like too much. So instead of creating a fabulous home that is reflective of the beauty inside you, you rob yourself of the satisfaction and pleasure that comes from living in YOUR authentic perfection.

You might even cop out and just rent a hotel suite to entertain--anything to avoid the feeling of shame that comes from not feeling perfect or good enough.

It is just not perfect.

If I ask, "What is perfect?" The answer I usually hear is, "In this magazine I saw this" or "On TV I saw that." That does not mean it is perfect. Those homes are staged and may not be set-up for real living. You get to define 'perfect' for yourself! If you had a museum 'perfect' home with everything in its place, it would feel very cold, unwelcoming and uncomfortable. You would not want to live in that space.

Why would you, as a strong woman, struggle with your own home? First, you have the pressure to be 'perfect', after all that is probably what advanced you to your successes in business. You also may judge yourself harshly, thinking that because you do not have the 'perfect' home, it is a negative reflection on you. You might even believe that you should know how to do everything yourself including interior design. You must be in control. But what follows that train of thought is a feeling of less than or even deeper: a sense of failure. There seems to be a little voice behind you saying, "There is a part of you where you are not good enough."

Sometimes the feeling of not good enough can be hidden behind over-achievement. Since there is so much in the creative process that is not concrete you cannot hide, leaving you feeling exposed.

Whether you are a homeowner of a large estate, smaller home or condo, it doesn't matter--there is always something you can do to elevate your enjoyment in your home. There is always possibility. Yet, sadly, we turn possibility into judgment about falling short of perfection. That not only makes it difficult to enjoy the home you have, it also makes it tough to discover what it is that you really want from your home.

Strong women judge themselves. We all do. I can not tell you how many of my clients totally rearranged, straightened up, or cleaned the entire house before my first meeting with them. When I arrived, I walked in ready to show what works for them and I noticed they had removed all the evidence I needed to see. I am there to help them live in their home more authentically expressing who they are, and to do it in a way that is more stylish and beautiful--in a way that is more reflective of them--in a way that is more organized, yet not in the unrealistic "everything is picture perfect" way.

The truth is, they are embarrassed. Here they are, powerful and successful women, and yet, they are actually embarrassed by the state of their homes as seen by a stranger they think is judging them. Many times their homes are beautiful. So why can't they see the beauty in their homes to start? Is it because they don't have a positive emotional connection to their home? Or, perhaps it does not reflect who they are or how they live. Instead they are busy comparing it to whatever was on the latest magazine cover and feeling they have come up short.

Comparison and competitiveness play a major role in the psyche of "women in charge". Often they are not aware of it. I get it. As the CEO of my own company, I too am a powerful woman. And I have the added pressure of being an interior designer! So if someone visits my home, I think I know what they expect to see. I have had to stop myself, "Wait a minute, Sheryl. What are you doing here? You love your home." It took me a while to design my home in a way that my husband and I would love.

Now, I live in a space that I really enjoy. There was a time when I kept asking myself, "Where are these expectations coming from?" Now I just hope that those who visit my home enjoy a wonderful space and a little bit of us.

So, I do understand why you may feel the pressure of competition, self-judgment, and even a little bit of shame, even though you have nothing to be ashamed of. It really is time to let it go and realize that with authentic emotional connection to your space, this uneasiness will disappear and in its place will be joy and delight. The process of design can help make that happen.

Why Some Female CEOs Have Trouble Hiring an Interior Designer

Developing trust is a major challenge in the designer-CEO relationship. Why? Because for it to work, you need to be vulnerable, and that is NOT how you achieved your success up to this point in your life.

You excel in almost every area of your life and to do this, you have trained yourself to be self-reliant, always in control, not to let go, and so necessarily not to trust others completely. Perhaps you struggle in a very competitive work environment. To trust another woman is a challenge because you may have competed with other women to get where you are.

If you over-rely on your strengths--what got you your executive position--you may not get to where you want to go regarding your home. As your designer, if I am to really understand you, I need to see things you may not want me to see. I need to talk with you and have deep conversations to discover who you are--really. I cannot just rely on what tidbits you throw my way. A good designer will pay attention to the details of your life without judging them. I pay attention to many things. I rely on my past experience in corporate America to bring in a new insight. Now that I am in a totally creative field, I listen with different ears.

The relationship between you and your designer should, by necessity, become a very intimate one. At the end of the day, your designer will not only have knowledge of your profession but most likely an understanding of your financial situation, marital relationship, and the overall temperament of everyone in your home. They may even know many of your insecurities. To create a space in which you will thrive, it is best to have that deeper relationship. I get vulnerable too. We both do.

Our relationship needs to work for both of us. In my case, my clients are not just choosing an interior designer; I am also choosing a client. Our relationship must be good and whole for both of us. We both need to be vulnerable so that you can let go of whatever prevents you from digging deep and discovering what you really want--not just what you have seen in the magazines, but what you really enjoy.

Obviously, this can get personal. This is why, as your designer, my highest priority is to develop trust. Trust is necessary for the process to work. For example, you need to feel confident that I will be a good steward and careful with your finances. There are two ways to ensure this will happen: First, a thorough Letter of Agreement that is accepted by both you and the designer. Not only does this legally protect both of you, but it also sets intentions clearly and defines what is everyone's role in the design process. Second, a complete budget is developed, including a percentage of set aside or 'just in case' money for any surprises that may come up. Just as in a marriage, poor communication and financial issues add strain if there is not a strong relationship, a level of trust, and a clear plan. One of my tasks as a designer is to give you, the client, the best recommendations possible based on the design and the budget. In short, you need a designer that only wants the best for you.

The Home Design Industry is somewhat responsible for the confusion clients have experienced in regard to interior design. Historically, only the very rich, the elite of the elite, could engage an architect or an interior designer for their home. This is how the industry came to be. Over time the demand and importance of good interior design evolved. The recognition that good design is for everyone started to take hold. During that time the industry was basically unregulated. There were and still are to this day some inconsistencies in how designers came to this profession. Many designers were educated through design certificate programs, undergraduate and graduate degrees. Others used their natural talents and were able to hone their path through apprenticeships and work experience. With time, some even became great designers.

Generally, designers that are formally trained hold themselves to a wider reach of standards, possibly higher standards. Each year they commit to continuing education to make sure that they know the industry codes and trends, and the newest methods, techniques and technology. Many interior designers are members of ASID (Association of Interior Designers). As the largest association of design professionals, the ASID oversees the licenses, guarantees the expertise, etc. Other organizations approach the industry differently.

The bottom line is that the industry is inconsistent in its approach to the profession, and that inconsistency can erode trust. If you have never engaged a designer, it is difficult to know what to expect. How can you know what something costs if there is no standard to go by? What is acceptable and what is not? If you are uncomfortable with these inconsistencies, you have reason to be.

This is especially difficult for female CEOs who want to be in control. As a strong woman leader, you excel at being in control. These women expertly solve problems. You typically do this based on information, statistics, or a set of past experiences. You establish norms so everything is predictable and it works.

Well, because there are no hard and fast guidelines in the interior design industry, and it being an unfamiliar area for most female CEOs, you find yourself in an uncomfortable situation. You do not have anything to go by and of course this makes you feel uneasy.

A good designer will provide you with a set of tools so that you know what to expect, so that you have a standard that you can count on. It does not have to be anyone else's standard. It can be a standard just for you—one that will guide you through the process, that will help you relate better with your designer, and that will help you to co-create with your designer.

You do not need to know where a sofa should be placed or what fabrics to choose. But you do need to feel comfortable with the process. You need to know that if something is placed in front of you and you experience a reaction to it, you can communicate that reaction. Any designer who is on point will be able to: first, recognize that there was a reaction and, second, discuss with you the source of the reaction. Sometimes it is not, "I do not like it." though those words might best express the feeling. Sometimes it is really, "I have never seen this before. Is this okay?" A designer should be able to notice the comment or question as a reaction and then engage in a conversation that unpacks what that really means.

I get reactions from my clients all the time. Some of the best designs I have ever created, designs my clients love, would never have gotten off the table if I had I presented the concept in the very first days of our relationship. It would not have happened because my client had not opened up enough. They were not yet willing and able to step into the unknown--to know if they really liked or did not like what was being presented. Plus, I could not assess their reaction at first. I have the most fun when we get to that level of openness. I love it.

You Are a Challenge!

Let's face it. You are not the easiest person with whom to work. In fact, you present a number of challenges for most designers.

One of the greatest challenges I find in working with female CEOs is that you are the ultimate decision maker and are not always available. You are either traveling or you are really busy. That can lead to you not being involved as much as needed in making decisions. This is a common problem, one that we need to address through our communication processes, or project time frame, or both.

A second challenge is that from time to time we will disagree. You will hear me say, "That is not going to work and give us the results you are seeking." or "I can't recommend this." As a design professional, I hold to certain design standards. If I am asked to do something that I know will not work, I have to say no. For example, I certainly will not implement anything against a building code. A code is law in my world and it is in place for the health and safety of all concerned. I also will not recommend anything that knowingly will not hold up under use.

Many powerful women are not used to someone saying no or disagreeing with them. They may be more accustomed to issuing directives and having others comply. When it comes to interior design, you do need to make all the key decisions,

BUT without the knowledge and expertise necessary, you are not in total control. For some that can be very disturbing.

In your business world, others expect you to be on top of your game and to know everything (even though it is impossible). You may find that you often deal with topics that you really know little about, and yet you become an authority quickly in order to make decisions. The business world and the creative world are often on the opposite ends of the spectrum, which brings me to another challenge. What I do is outside your area of expertise and you may not automatically see the whole picture. I find that this can make a woman in charge a little uneasy and uncomfortable. If this is not addressed early, it affects the trust level needed for success. The worst thing that could happen is for your designer to let these issues slide, putting the whole project in jeopardy of falling apart.

Another challenge I have encountered is the very guarded CEO. This may be necessary in business life especially if you are working in a very competitive world--a world where openness and vulnerability is seen as weakness. In the world of design, vulnerability is a window into who we really are, our authentic selves. When I get to peek through that window I can see my client a little clearer. One of the least satisfying things that I could do as a designer is to design a home for someone based on the facade they present. The design itself becomes just a facade. It may not serve the client's needs. It is just for show--pretty, but a place usually lacking any emotional connection. Possibly, denying them an opportunity to live in a place they really enjoy and love. If they do not enjoy it, they will either neglect or avoid it altogether.

It sounds odd but it is very common to have rooms in your home that you have not lived in for years. These rooms could be filled with very expensive furnishings, beautiful accents, and "designer" touches. Is it possible that you just do not like these rooms? Or, perhaps in those spaces you don't feel connected? If you enjoy a space, you will find a reason to be in that space. If you are avoiding (consciously or unconsciously) a room, then it is just like having wasted space. It is not serving you well.

When trust issues emerge, I try to address them immediately. One thing that many powerful CEOs have in common is the ability to resolve issues quickly. If trust issues are not addressed immediately, it can lead to anxiousness and sometimes blindly making decisions too quickly.

At the start of my career I was hired to design a beautiful home for a powerful woman in charge. She actually warned me that she might have a "few" trust issues. All my suggestions and recommendations were always being challenged, though I was giving her exactly what she wanted. At some point the realities of what it takes to create a custom design and custom furnishings set in. She became very uncomfortable with not being in total control over the process and the time frame. Throughout the project she stopped the job several times and even replaced the contractors a couple of times. Because of all the trust issues the project was extended two times longer than planned and ended up costing three times more. The project did result in a beautiful home but at a much greater expense to my client than it would have been had the trust issues been addressed early. Now my insistence on addressing these difficult issues early in the design process keeps us all at 100%. That doesn't mean there are no challenges along the way. It means that the handling of all the challenges that come up just became easier with better results.

A Gift for You

For your complimentary *Design•ology Checklist:*

How to Hire a Designer That Will Work For YOU, visit

www.designologybook.com

The Design Effect

d randolph foulds photography

What Makes You Smile?

I ask you: when are you truly relaxed and enjoying yourself? Think about those times when you feel that there is just nothing but beauty around you. When and where does this happen for you?

Is it when you first walk into your home? Or do you feel that sense of total relaxation and comfort only when you are on a vacation? Do you have to leave your home to find that sense of peace for a week? Two weeks? What if you could experience this feeling every day? I love vacations too--going to a faraway island and spending time at a resort by the beach. I love all of that. I love it not just because of its natural beauty, but because it is peaceful and it allows me to relax totally.

Would you want that feeling every single day? What if you could walk into your home and say, "Wow! I am vacationing at home right now"? Wouldn't that be wonderful? What if that becomes part of your daily routine? Would that give you something to look forward to?

I want this for you. I want you to look forward to being at home at the end of the day and saying: "Oh my God, I am going home. This is wonderful."

Just imagine your husband or your significant other has prepared a fantastic meal. They call you and say: "Do not worry about anything, just come home. I have it all taken care of." What if you could experience this feeling everyday? How would that change your life?

A great interior designer can help you accomplish this in two major ways.

First, they can help you narrow down and discover exactly what you want from your home because you do not often think about it. What is it that you want? What is it that really makes you smile? What is it that makes you happy? What is it that makes you giggle?

Second, they can help you notice the difference between what you want and what you do not want. What is it that is being forced on you? For example, if you had total control over everything in your life, what would you exclude? It may be part of something you are required to deal with. Wouldn't it be nice if you didn't have to deal with that at all? Wouldn't it be great if you could really truly control your environment so that it is exactly what you want it to be?

A good designer can help you do that.

Many times I help my clients discover who they really are. It can be surprising because you may have a lot of "shoulds" in your life--rules and regulations about what you should do and what you shouldn't do. All of this is swarming in your head.

One of my clients once said, "Well, I work in a very conservative and rigid environment and so this is what my home is supposed to look like." Then she went on to say my style is this, my colors are this, not too loud or not too out there. But after working together, I discovered she was not like that at all. She was actually fun to be with, loved colors, and enjoyed texture. She loved playfulness and creativity, but she had never allowed herself to think about those things. She was finally able to get away from the "shoulds" and "shouldn'ts" and start enjoying life in the moment!

So, when I pose questions to you as my client, I want you to think about this: What do you want? What is it you want to experience? Who are you? What are you all about? Help me create a perfect environment for you.

I remember two of my favorite clients—a couple which were just so willing and open. They actually taught me everything that I needed to know about interior design. They were both high-powered CEOs. Both were very busy people with huge demands at work, especially in the form of travel. They basically met each other every weekend at their home because they were on the road all week.

I designed their family room and kitchen. When we finished, they said, "We love to be in this room together. We just sit and smile. We feel so good and we just enjoy the idea of us being in this beautiful space." They spent more time together just to be in that space!

I love my work.

Another favorite client of mine is a very strong and high level VP, busy but once again, very open. I created a home design for her 7,800 square foot house where she lives alone. She lives in each and every room in her home. She would say "Today I am going to be in this room; it is so beautiful. I feel peaceful in this room and in this other room I feel energized." I love her. I love that she enjoys her home and that each space is an adventure for her. It is not a showcase--it is all for her and yes, when people come over, they are amazed. While she appreciates their compliments, their reaction was not the intent of the design--it was just one of the outcomes. The intent was for her to truly feel that her home is her place to be.

Many of my clients find they are extremely satisfied beyond their expectations because they did not realize how much they needed such a space in their life. It wasn't until they actually got it.

I hear: "This is it. This is so good. This is wonderful."

Why is it Important to Hire a Designer?

Your ideal designer will offer you the opportunity to look inside yourself and find the joy that is missing or bring out more of the joy that is apparent.

What is that joy that you want to tap into? The design process is a chance to express yourself in a way you have not done so before. You have an opportunity to be in your home as who you truly are, authentically, without any pressure, competition, or judgment. Imagine that!

When you hire the right designer, you are bringing into your life a professional who can help you get to the core of what will make your home a beautiful, warm, inviting environment--a place that is going to help you reach some of your goals. Goals like being more productive or feeling more loved. It may sound woo-woo but it is not. After all, this is your home. This is what holds you. You are the precious cargo so your home needs to nourish you. It really needs to make you smile. Hiring a professional who knows this, is trained, and has done it before is very important.

Why hire a professional designer? There are many reasons to do so. Here are the top five as highlighted on Houzz.com, a website dedicated to helping you find the right interior designer:

(1) You will save time.

You will absolutely save time but where you save time is even more important. The duration of the project is fixed, based on what is the actual project. That is not where you save the most time. You save time in the exploration phase when you are discovering what you want. You also save time in finding the items you need.

You could spend endless hours shopping retail only to find what you thought was unique is really one of many. As a successful woman in charge, you deserve to surround yourself with those things that were customized for you alone. Shopping retail (only) is also very limiting as to what is being sold in your region. Most established interior designers have relationships directly with manufacturers, artisans and design centers. There are some exceptions in the retail industry that provide designer (to the trade) programs, so that designers can service their clients with customized items locally. Since your designer is doing all the footwork and bringing those custom items directly to you, a great deal of time is saved. Searching for just the right piece by visiting store after store can be a total waste of time.

A terrific designer is someone who is constantly evolving coming from both head and heart. As long as your designer is creating from the heart not just the head, you will find someone who is willing to be more transformative or enlightened in their design approach. They are most likely more in touch with who they are, therefore, can help you better discover who you are. In my work, I bring all my experiences and education to every project. Not just what I know about the principles of design but what I have learned and experienced through years of travel, working with people from all over the world, enjoying the different cultures, architecture, fashion, foods, music and dance, as well as my growth through working in the corporate environment.

When you allow yourself the luxury of customized furniture you need a creative professional designer. It is so nice, no matter how small, to have someone design a totally customized piece of furniture just for you. For example, a chair made to your personalized specifications--the perfect chair with a great design, made of the right materials, specific pitch, certain lean, a particular seat and of course the right fabric. You need a professional to do that. In this respect, especially at the beginning of the design process, you save massive amounts of time. It is impossible to retail shop for an item that has not been created yet.

Most CEOs don't have the time or expertise to manage a construction project but, believe it or not, some still try. They know of a 'good' contractor or handyman that did some work for a friend or neighbor. They have an idea of what they think a design should be. They are assured that exactly what they want can be done. They are so excited about the cost not realizing that there is a reason, or let me say a price you pay, for the cost being so low. They don't ask to see construction plans or drawings or in some cases evidence of past work or references. They don't mind that the contractor is not licensed because "they did a really good job for a friend". Stop it! Doing this is not a good idea.

Working with an experienced design professional saves you a mountain of aggravation and time by avoiding expensive mistakes in the area of building codes and best practices. On a practical level, this means that you won't have walls falling down. When a professional designer is designing a space, it is in the context of the total impact on your home.

(2) You will benefit from the designer's expertise and understanding of the overall construction process.

This is essential, especially if you have never gone through construction before. You need your designer to sit down and educate you about the construction process. There are always surprises. If somebody tells you there are not going to be any surprises, be wary. You will want to know: when do the surprises usually occur, what are some of the alternatives, and who can handle them?

In construction, there is an element of the unknown. You are going to enlarge a room so you open up a wall. Who knew that there is asbestos in this wall that should not be there and it has been there for 20 years! For example, I was working on a basement. We were just finishing the changing out the flooring. The old flooring comes up and who knew? We discovered asbestos underneath the floor and had been disturbed during the construction. The job stops. What do you do? A HAZMAT crew is brought in to remove the asbestos. Nobody can touch it. Your contractor cannot clean it up unless he is licensed in that area. I have seen people who are inexperienced attempting to cover it up, bad idea, and illegal.

I have come in on jobs where the previous homeowner may not have used a professional designer or contractor and many of the 'improvements' were not up to code. Codes deal with fire, health and safety. These include making sure that the air is healthy, making sure that you are not contributing to off-gassing of certain materials, using surfaces that create a healthy environment for your family. All of this is essential.

Knowing and understanding codes is especially important because your architect and contractor are legally required to meet the local codes. When your project involves new construction the execution of that project requires a team effort. A great designer not only understands the codes but also can use that knowledge to create more possibilities. So you want a designer that will make that process smoother by being a good team player.

For higher-end projects, with more complex building codes, consider engaging a more skilled professional—one with both architecture and design training.

(3) A designer speaks the language.

Designers speak many languages. They speak their client's language--your language. They speak the language of the design industry. They speak the language of the contractor.

As an architect-designer, I also speak the language of the architect. With many different terminologies in a project, there needs to be a translator. I find that the layman does not speak the same language as the construction professionals that are implementing the project. Your designer is your translator, your advocate.

(4) You benefit from their design talent and attention to detail.

It's all in the details. True. No matter how simple a design, one little detail can make a world of difference. If I design a kitchen, perhaps that detail is to offset the cabinets a couple of inches. If I get this detail wrong, it causes such havoc that a whole row of cabinets needs to come out. The details are what make a design beautiful and what distinguish the designer from a do-it-yourselfer.

(5) You receive greater access to other skilled professionals.

When you hire a designer you hire a team. You hire tradesmen and artisans that the designer has worked with on other projects. These relationships are invaluable. Designers work with different contractors and their subcontractors all the time, so they generally know who does a good job and how well they manage their projects. If you ask me to recommend contractors, I usually give you a list of two or three recommendations--people that I trust can do the job, do it well, and do it professionally. All are contractors who are licensed, reliable, great team players in solving problems, and very skilled. Then I encourage you to interview the contractors and make your decision.

How to Turn Your Home into Your Happy Place

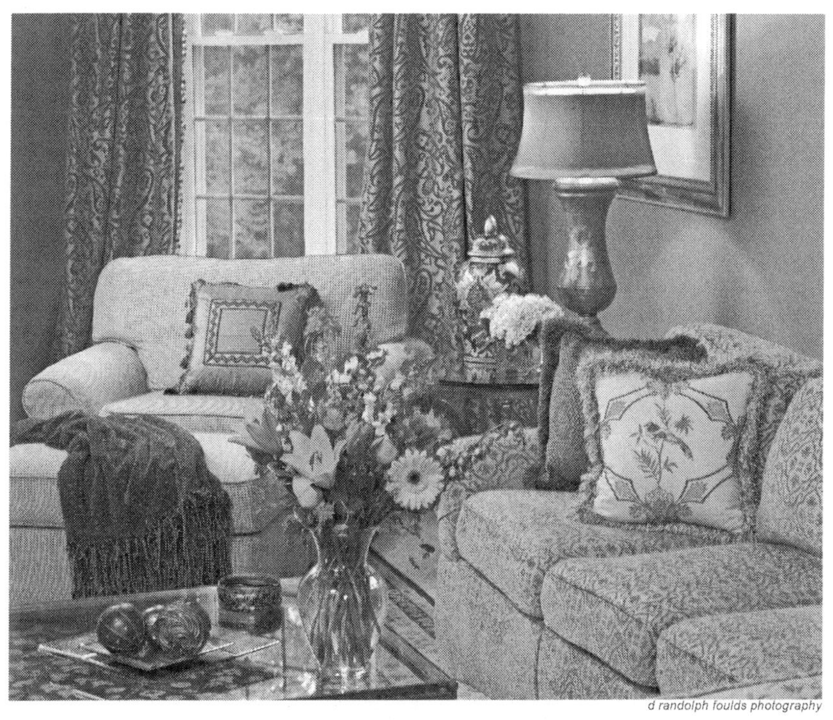

d randolph foulds photography

What is the Designer's Role?

My role as a designer begins before the design phase. It starts by listening and communicating with my clients, learning about their needs and desires. After establishing an open trusting relationship and accessing where I can be of most service, only then can I start to plan a design. It is then that the design development begins, which includes measuring, research, layouts, making selections, designing pieces of furniture and creating drawings and construction documents. On a very large project, I usually do all the initial schematic drawings, and then send them out to a production team in the final design phase to produce more detail renderings, which will save time and therefore my client money.

After the design is developed and approved, then comes implementation. There are two parts to implementation: construction and purchasing of the furnishings.

Construction needs project management or oversight—working with your general contractor to implement the design. How will the process unfold? How many days will it take? Who are all the players? What are all the steps involved? Construction is coordinated between the designer and the contractor or the architect.

Your designer oversees the construction realities in respect to the approved design. They bring project feedback to you so that you are constantly informed about the progress (or lack thereof) and any issues that come up. Your designer is your liaison and advocate, thus saving you time and aggravation. While the construction phase is underway, the coordination of the purchasing of key design elements, such as flooring, window treatments, furniture, lighting and accessories is taking place.

Throughout the process, your designer is your financial steward. A considerable amount of money is involved in any interior design project—much of it placed down ahead of delivery, sometimes hundreds of thousands of dollars. Your designer always keeps the measure, with check and balance, between what goes to this category, what goes to that category. Your designer keeps you informed and updated.

What is Your Role in the Design Process?

Be Open

As a homeowner, your first role would be to remain open to your designer using their expertise to assess the possibilities. Being open can be a little uncomfortable for the powerful decision maker who wants to always be in control. It is in this discovery phase that your designer is looking at your project from totally different points of view. Perhaps, a view you never considered. This means that you will need to be open to the designer's recommendations and assessments.

After speaking with many of my colleagues, I have concluded that most welcome their clients' involvement. A collaborative design usually has the greatest results. There is a point, however, where you as a client can get in the way. Let me be clear, as the client you have total control over what you want and what you are purchasing. But, when we are in that unknown zone, to overreact and circumvent the process is never good. As an experienced designer myself, I usually identify if we are approaching that point. So I am in the camp of good communications. Conveying to you what is happening, what it's going to cost, and how it's going to unfold is important.

When you are in the middle of a project, I doubt that you want to deliberately stop the process or shut things down. When that occurs, you need to sit down and have a conversation with your designer and get some clarity and understanding of what is happening. Things come up in any project; this is why it is so important to trust your designer and have a designer that knows what they are doing.

You want to hire a designer that is not intimidated by you. When issues arise, decisions have to be made--sometimes on the spot. You need your designer to be in tune with who you are. Of course, if it is a financial decision, a designer, as a good steward of your money, will need to get you involved right away. For example, I would say, "Okay, this is what has come up. These are the financial consequences to this or that situation. One of these must be chosen today."

One of your responsibilities is not only to be open but also to handle your end of the financial agreement. As a designer, I have experienced situations where I was assured that all the resources were available, and this turned out not to be the case. We initiated the job, only to find that money for phase one was in the bank, but there was no money available for the second phase. This meant the job needed to be shut down and later restarted. Most people do not understand how this business works. They think, "Oh, we are just shutting it down until Friday. Next Friday I will be back in town and I will deal with it then. That is only a week." A week to client might be a month to me because the construction team has other commitments they have to keep. They may have to leave the project for a while because of the change in schedule and their commitments to other projects.

Making sure that everybody is on point contractually, especially with the finances, is key.

Again, I return to trust. In these situations, as your designer, I am responsible. I trust you and you need to trust me. After all, I have the keys to your house. I may need to have access when you are not at home. Trust and openness is vital.

Always Communicate Before You Act

"One small change…."

I walked into the home after completing a full living room design and to my surprise my clients were redoing their floors! They decided that since they were doing all this other work, they might as well install hardwood floors. Their thought was, "Well, she is buying new furniture, so while she is doing that let's rip up the carpet and put in hardwood floors." They did not communicate with me, so they did not consider that the color palette and the furnishing selections were built into their design based on the existing carpet. Now we have to reselect. Not good. Not good at all.

Situations like this are even more challenging because, like most designers, I work on several projects simultaneously. I might work on four or five projects at once with two other projects in the wings that start in a few weeks. Now I need to redo the whole design package while initiating the next project. The result? We may need to lengthen the time required for your project significantly because I may not be able to return to your design until after I start this other project. My commitment to other clients is now a factor.

And since you already signed off on your design, I was able to make that commitment. The items that are chosen in the redo may be backordered seriously delaying delivery, and there is extra expense in design time. You can see the whole domino effect when sudden design changes just show up.

Expect the Unexpected

I commissioned a sectional from a very reputable and excellent custom furniture maker—someone I had worked with for a while and whom I knew would do a beautiful job. My client was trying to get the living room ready for holiday entertaining. They spent most of their time in the family room. No one paid attention to what was happening to the living room sectional. About three or four weeks before the party, my client sat on the sectional and noticed that it felt like the cushion inside had started to shrink. The foam inside the seat cushion seemed to begin to crumble.

Now, when someone calls me about a piece of furniture that is only two months old and tells me that all the cushions are crumbling, it just doesn't make sense. So here I am trying to figure out what was going on. I could see that the fabric and the casing around the cushion were bunching up. Whatever was supporting the fabric had shriveled up and the rest was just hanging off.

"What happened?" I'm thinking, "Did I use the wrong fabric?" At first, I thought perhaps the fabric had stretched. Now this is a $10,000 sectional and the client is not happy.

So I say, "Okay. It looks like the fabric stretched but usually if fabric stretches, it tends to stretch in all directions, not in only one direction." I was mystified. So I called the manufacturer. (I am so glad that I have good relationships with the manufacturers.) They requested I send one of the complete covered cushions back to them at their cost. They said, "Just overnight it and we will figure this out." So I did.

The next day I got a call telling me that there is good news and more good news. The first good news was the very quick diagnosis of cushion failure from the foam manufacturer. The second good news was that there was an immediate solution. I FedEx all the covered cushions back to the workroom. They had it taken care of in a week and a half, to the delight of my client!

It all worked out. Sometimes one just has to have a sense of humor and expect the unexpected. Stuff does happen.

Be Involved in the Design Process

How involved should you be? It depends on the project and how involved you want to be. As a designer, I never mix professionals with do-it-yourselfers, especially if there is a construction component. For me, everybody must be experienced, trained, licensed, and insured. I need to know that everything will be done professionally and that it is going to be done right. That is the only way that I will handle a design project.

If you want to be involved in the design process, you could hire your designer to only research and make all the selections of furniture and color palette. Leaving you to implement the plan. If you hire them to do this, yet you decide to 'help' by taking on the task of finding all the furnishings on your own while emailing questions everyday asking their opinion, you are not just involved. You are actually doing the job you hired your designer to do. Normally, when this occurs there will be conflict. Your designer has already mapped out the project based on an understanding of who you are, your lifestyle, what you have requested, and the budget. If you don't trust your designer to use their expertise to complete the project then I suggest that you not hire that designer. Do not treat your designer as a personal shopper. You can find a shopping expert for far less money to purchase your request. Here is where I say, "Stop it." You are shortchanging yourself and not benefiting from your designer's expertise.

Early in the process, before I even begin the design, we discuss where we are going with the design. You share with me the things you like and show me examples. After that you need to turn it over to me, your designer. Otherwise, it just does not work.

One of the luxuries of hiring a designer is having somebody who knows you, is there for you, knows the industry, knows the world of design, knows what is available and knows what works. Your designer is going to bring that knowledge to you so that you do not have to spend hours and hours looking for it. Your designer is doing considerable research so that you don't have to. It is such an advantage, such a luxury, to have someone do this work for you. Sit back, relax, and enjoy it. You will be better off and will be much happier at the end.

Conflicts and Surprises

d randolph foulds photography

The Recliner

Many designers agree: there is one piece of furniture we would never have designed or created: the lazy man chair or, as it is better known, the recliner.

Perhaps it is because the recliner brings back images of the late 1960's and the chair of choice in the 1970 sitcom, "All in the Family". It was the first accessory piece to the true "man cave". You just flop into this chair. It is very comfortable, but it is like a black sea. Designers (including me) spend considerable research time trying to find a recliner that has all the comfort levels of your typical recliner but does not look like a recliner.

As designers we notice certain things when we meet with clients for the first time. Some of these trigger red flags and the whistles go off in our heads. One is the husband saying, " I have got to have a recliner."

Actually, I have been blessed to discover a couple of furniture makers that design beautiful recliners that look like sculptural modern pieces. Then, voila! You push a button and it becomes a recliner. This discovery was the only way that I could deal with incorporating a recliner into a design.

"The Recliner" is an example of a nightmare scenario that we, as designers, deal with all the time. It is funny because sometimes, the designer does not win. Sometimes, they say, "Okay, if you have to have a recliner it just can't look like the armchair that Archie Bunker use to have." I hear this story all this time. And the fact is, most people do not believe that I can choose a chair and ottoman that is actually more comfortable and gives you more back support than that recliner-- where you just slump in and become just like a dead whale.

Can you tell that I do not like the look of typical recliners? I get that people think they are comfortable. Unfortunately, many manufacturers haven't invested in improving their design to make them also beautiful. Whatever the piece of furniture, it needs to be stylish and attractive. It should fit into the décor in beautiful fabrics and leathers. They should not be so over-scaled that they take over the room. These are the tips your interior designer would help you resolve.

The 60-inch Television

I've presented the design. The room is gorgeous. It is everything the client could want in the room. Then I hear the dreaded question: "Wow! Even though this is all beautiful, how is my 60-inch TV screen going to fit?"

Now, the easiest solution is to put the desired flat screen over the fireplace. Design Tip: Usually, what makes a design work well is having one focal point in the room. Everything else is subordinate and supports that focal point. That makes for a very cohesive environment. It is very different from walking into a room where you have a gorgeous fireplace and a beautiful view and then, BOOM, a 60-inch flat screen all vying for your attention. "Okay, who is number one and who is number two or three?"

Oftentimes, the battle is between the couple. One of them wants the TV; the other one wants the fireplace or the view. I try to play referee (not always a good idea). Sometimes, I am successful. I remind people that the real estate they paid for was really about the view. The fireplace could be considered secondary because that is an architectural element that is permanent to the house. Then there is the TV. I don't always win, but for the sake of the design it's worth a try.

What I attempt to do in situations like this is give everybody all the elements they want. There are fun ways to hide the TV: pop-up out of a console or possibly hide the screen behind wall cabinets.

A solution I really love is to have a print produced of their favorite painting in an oversize format and put it in a remote controlled picture frame box installed in front of a wall hung flat screen TV. When you want to see the TV, using the remote control the canvas goes up into the picture frame and you have a full view of the TV. When the canvas goes down and you have a beautiful framed work of art. So much fun! In a contemporary space, I designed a mirrored wall and the TV is actually in the mirror. The only drawback with this approach is that the manufacturers haven't developed the mirror option to the point where they can accommodate a 60-inch screen.

I always look for ways to hide these screens so they do not become the focal point in a room unless it is a theater room. Often, I have witnessed husband and wife, or a partner and partner, in battle over which design element is going to be the priority. To make it worse, throw in the recliner. Sometimes, I just have to laugh because it can be a real point of conflict. People get attached to things and it is really difficult to help them open up to possibilities that they really might enjoy. It can be challenging for sure.

Pets

Pets can make for interesting situations. Most people have pets. We love our dogs and we love our cats. We all know that they can be extremely destructive.

One of my clients called and she said, "Oh my God. The chair that you ordered is all shredded." Perplexed I asked "What do you mean shredded?" She said, “The fabric is unraveling!”

"What?" I thought, “What happened?” I would not believe the answer if I had not seen it myself. There was a piece of exposed thread on the bottom of this skirted chair and her very cute and curious puppy had been picking and picking and picking until he pulled enough of the thread that he could actually hold it in his mouth. Then he ran around and around and around the chair with the thread.

Each time he went around the chair, he was actually pulling the thread out of the fabric. Eventually, all that left was the wool yarn all the way up, 19 inches from the floor, only three weeks after the chair had been installed. We would never have figured out how it happened except the puppy came in with his tail wagging and a broken piece of thread hanging from his mouth. All you could say was, "Oh my God. This doggie has unraveled all of this fabric to just strings." It was funny until the manufacturer refused to cover the loss because it was the client's responsibility to train her dog, even a puppy.

A Big Mistake

An important and expensive project coupled with a year-end party deadline… what could go wrong? We selected a beautiful, imported silk fabric, very difficult to get, hand-beaded, the crème de la crème for custom window treatments! I use several different workrooms from time to time, but in this case I selected one that I was very confident would do superb work. They have always done an excellent job. My client was hosting a party at the year-end and it was very important that we finish in time.

Because of the lead-time on all the imported items, the last thing that needed to be finished was the window treatments. The fabric finally arrived and I had the eight weeks I needed for completion. Eight weeks for the workroom to fabricate what I had designed for two extremely large windows--twenty feet high and probably ten feet wide. I was so excited. The effect of walking into a room and seeing the grandeur of twenty feet of this most beautiful hand-beaded fabric would be spectacular.

I received the window treatments on time. Everything was on schedule. Everyone was ready: my assistants, my installer, and me. Together, we were ready to go in and stage it. This was going to be beautiful. We were actually way ahead of schedule--three or four weeks before the grand party.

Yes, we were ready

I opened up the box and looked at the fabric. The way it was made was so perfect, with one significant exception: the beautiful, hand-beaded window treatments measured nine-feet tall and I had specified twenty-feet tall!

I cried for a full hour.

After my big cry, I still did not know how to resolve this nightmare. Now, I was under the gun. I reached out to the workroom. They, of course, were very apologetic but that did not make a difference. No matter what it takes we have to work twenty-four seven to resolve this. One option would be to order more of the fabric and do a complete re-make. We could have it done except the fabric was back ordered which meant there was not enough time. The fabric itself would not be available for another three months.

I could not select a different fabric because it was integrated into other areas of the design. The fabric coordinated with all the other elements. Thank God I sent the correct yardage needed for the original design to the workroom.

So I just took out my pencil and paper and said, "How can you design a very large drapery with what amounted to pieces of fabric'? I redesigned the whole thing, added some gorgeous trim to cover seams, and had the workroom also change out the lining.

They did it! They turned it around in two weeks. My stomach was in my chest, then in my throat. "What is it going to look like?" Then I opened the box. I have to say it was gorgeous - by far one of my best custom drapery designs. My clients were delighted. And I threw a huge party for my staff.

The angels were with me that day. Mistakes like this do happen. This is one time where a mistake was made and everything worked out. Anybody can make a mistake, even a great designer; the important thing is how one resolves it.

Six Questions NOT to Ask Your Interior Designer (But Everyone Does)

d randolph foulds photography

"What is Your Style?"

Many clients ask me about my style. I get this question all the time.

And no, I don't believe that this is a good question to ask when looking for a designer. Here is why: the design process is about discovering YOUR style not mine. Be wary of the designer that advertises a certain style. I don't--because the design is about you, not me.

Of course, I influence your design. I can't help but do that. But instead of exploring my personal style, which really has very little to do with your style, I'd rather we talk about certain things that I do that are consistent in my design. One of the things that I do is mix things up. I like to use a little bit of old and a little bit of new. I enjoy making some elements look as though they have been here for a while and will be there forever.

A better question to ask: "Tell me about your approach to my design."

When I work with a contemporary client, I might incorporate a couple of vintage pieces in their design. When I work with someone that is very traditional, I may introduce some contemporary art in their design. It keeps the spaces fresh and more interesting. That is something that is consistent in my design philosophy. But my personal style, I will never tell. My own style is a secret!

"How Do You Get Paid?"

If a client asks me early in the initial interview, "How are you getting paid?" what are they really asking or saying? They could be letting me know they do not trust me yet. They don't know if I am going to be a good steward of their money.

Yes, it is a trust issue.

Asking a designer " How do you get paid?" has very little to do with what the designer is charging you. While these questions are commonly asked, they are not good questions for a couple of reasons.

First, these questions do not get to the heart of what you really need to know: what is the designer charging you for their services? Are you getting your money's worth? And can you trust this designer to be a good steward of your resources?

Second, for most professionals, "how do you get your money?" is a slightly rude question. Where else do you ask that question? You do not go to a lawyer and say, "Well, how do you get your money?" You do not go to a doctor and ask, "Well, how do you get paid?" These are not the questions that you ask a professional. At the very least it shows a lack of understanding of their role and value in the process, which is not a good way to build trust in a new relationship. They will patiently answer the question, of course, but there are more respectful ways to ask what you really want to know.

A better question would be, "What are your fees?"

There are several ways that designers ask for their fees. Personally, I do most of my business with what is called a fixed fee. When I am assessing a job, I price the job based on what's going to be involved, how much experience and what level of expertise is required for me to complete the task.

A better question is: "What is this going to cost me?" That is a fair question. It is up to the designer to tell you their fees and if you need further explanation, they should explain why. One of the most difficult things to understand in this process, especially if you have never used a designer, is the separation between the design and implementation phase. As a result, there are usually two fees involved. First, for the design phase, which includes the pre-planning, the floor and furniture plan, the custom designed furniture and cabinetry, the construction docs, drawings or renderings, the furniture selections, and all of the research. Second, for the project management, purchasing and implementation of the design.

The design fee is based on the designer's expertise, experience, and level of education. All of that goes into how that designer determines their fees including what the market will bear in their geographic areas. In New York, for instance, you may have designers that charge $350 per hour and up on the high-end projects. You have some that charge $500 an hour. For some they react by saying, "Oh my God, that is so much." That means very little if it is not put into perspective. That is why I do not like to quote hourly fees for the design process. Some designers prefer hourly fees. I do not.

One reason I like to quote a fixed fee is that once I interview the client and know what the job entails, I can determine based on my experience, what this job is going to require and the level of expertise needed. From there, I calculate a fixed fee and quote it. That quote has nothing to do with the construction or purchasing of any products or materials. It applies to only the custom design.

When I give my clients a fixed fee it takes away the anxiety and opens up to more excitement. At the start they can relax and know how much of an investment is required. They feel comfortable knowing their designer is not going to nickel and dime them. This comfort level does not happen with only a straight hourly-fee model. When construction, project oversight or add-ons to the letter of agreement are involved, I do mix the fixed fee with hourly fees. When that happens I make sure my clients agree and approve the additional fees as well as understand what they are paying for and why.

Each designer has a business model they prefer. I developed my model based on my years of experience.

The proper question is not how you get paid but what are your fees.

"Why Does A Design Cost So Much?"

This can be a good or a bad question, but is usually the latter. It is certainly a multi-faceted question and its value depends on why you are asking it.

If you ask me "why does it cost so much" and you are asking about the design phase, the answer is simple: your price is based on a number of things. How many designer assistants are involved? How much time it will take to actually produce what you want? How much research is involved to get the products that you really desire? How much of the furniture, millwork and cabinetry is total custom design? How much experience does the designer have?

For example, I am an experienced specialist with a Master's degree in Architecture. I've been doing this a long time, so I have earned the right to say, "Okay. This is what I am worth."

Designer price ranges differ, and much of the difference is relative. The fact is, while you may feel that a project design costs too much, in reality it may not cost enough, especially if you factor into the design fee all the variables.

However, many times when that question comes up, and it does often, it comes with a hidden agenda. I would have to ask: "What's going on? What is it that you really want to know?" If I tell you why something costs a certain amount, does it clarify anything? It does not change the price, so that answer is only going to satisfy the person who is generally curious. But if you have some ulterior motive, a trust issue or confusion that needs clarification, my answer to that question may not help you. Suffice it to say that most of the time, if you ask "why does it cost so much" we will need to get the bottom of why you asked me the question in the first place.

Most of the time, it is a trust issue. As a client, you may not have anything to gauge against; you may have never worked with a designer; and you do not want to be cheated. Most people do not want to be ripped off, but at the same time want to be fair to all concerned. The problem is you do not know what is fair if you have never gone through this process. There is a lot going on when I see this question. So I get really honest and transparent with my clients and tell them exactly why it costs what it costs.

I want to skip lightly to the money talk. Since we are talking about finances, is this an area that challenges your comfort zone? Some of my clients have expressed a fear of losing control of money, power and sometimes their identity in the whole process. Usually, this is code for 'it is going to cost too much' or 'this might be more than I am comfortable spending'. I certainly believe working from a realistic budget is key to a positive outcome. But I am hearing the resistance before we are even talking about numbers. There are a lot of assumptions being made.

We have all had different paths to success. Some have had to climb the rough side of the mountain with many sacrifices and struggles, especially in finances. Others have had a much easier climb. Through all of it we develop habits and our own principles to live by. Maybe when you were struggling early in your career you could not afford some of the nicer things in life. But once you have arrived to a place where monies are available to you, giving yourself permission to step up and purchase the things you work so hard for, is difficult for some 'women in charge'. Being frugal is an admired trait to some, it is a conscious choice based on your value system. If that is important to my client I will always respect that and will work to support that ideal in my suggestions and recommendations. Being cheap is a reaction, usually from the past. I found that it has nothing to do with your principles as much as it is about fear. What comes to mind is fear and trust cannot share the same space. Fear is often a bad habit. Sometimes it is difficult to trust that you deserve the things you dreamed of having.

"Can you just give me some ideas?"

Or alternatively: Can we just sit down so I can pick your brain?

If you are paying for a consultation and you ask your designer, "Will you give me some ideas?" you are perfectly within your rights. You are paying for that service, those ideas. Now, keep in mind, you probably only have an hour or so. There are only so many ideas you are going to get and they are probably not going to be fully explored. Your designer hasn't measured your room yet or asked you all the appropriate questions. At this point, you are just floating ideas. It might not even be the ideas that will be settled on in the end. They are just ideas to be explored further.

For you to ask a designer to come in and give you ideas and not pay for the consultation is totally unacceptable. You are asking a professional, who has worked very hard, to essentially give away their expertise. It devalues your relationship with your designer. If your designer says yes, they would be devaluing themselves and disrespecting their profession. There is a big difference between doing it yourself and hiring a professional. Professionals get paid for their services. They have earned it.

"Do you receive discounts from the stores or manufacturers?"

I sometimes get this question. A better question would be, "Am I going to get a discount or a reduction compared to what the retailers charge?" My relationship with manufacturers and vendors is by way of my contract with them. It does not necessarily have anything to do with my contract with the client. If you ask me this question, I suspect that what you really want to know is how is this going to affect you? Are you going to receive a lower cost? What happens between me and the manufacturers and vendors is business between us.

I am tempted to respond, "Why are you asking that?" You would not go into a retail store, for example, Nordstrom's, and ask, "Did you get a discount when you bought this dress from the manufacturers because you bought a large quantity of them? Since you got a really good deal you should pass that discount off to me." One does not have anything to do with the other. That is my "slap-in-the-face" answer. Bam-bam-bam. All jokes aside, a better question is to ask if there are any cost saving measures that can be considered?

"Can You Complete my Design Before the Wedding?" (Or Party...?)

Early in my career as a designer, I encountered a situation that taught me a great deal. My client was preparing for a huge party and I was a new designer. It seemed like a reasonable amount of time for me to pull this dining room together. It was going to be a fabulous dining room and everything was selected. The design portion went smoothly.

Then things changed. It started with the manufacturer putting the wallpaper we chose on a six-week backorder. Next, some selections of the furniture were backordered. Backorder essentially means those products are not available because they need more quantity to be fabricated or they are out of the country and the shipping times are weeks or even months out. This could happen at anytime, even a day after you have specified those items. When the trucking company finally delivers the furniture to my receiver, he calls me and says, "We have some trucking damage." This all happened three weeks out from our anticipated installation date. We had already been waiting weeks for this furniture.

My client was expecting fifty people at the party and now we didn't have wallpaper or all the furniture. Yikes! All I could do was temporarily take my designer hat off and put on a party planner hat. So I said "Okay, this is what we are going to do. It is the best that we can do. We are going to rent some tables and bring in rental chairs. I am going to decorate this so nobody even realizes that they have been rented."

We brought in beautiful fabrics, tablecloths, lots of candles, and tablescape. We used buckets of fresh flowers and decorated our hearts out. We did everything we could do to make the place fabulous. And it was! Even though my client held her breath the entire time, everyone said, “This is so beautiful." I hid underneath the table figuratively. I was so scared, but it worked out beautifully. The room was gorgeous.

Sometime things like this happen and, at the end of the day, one just has to laugh. There was nothing else we could do about it. Needless to say, I no longer promise a project will be completed for a specific event or holiday.

In a perfect world, your designer can give you the exact date your project will be finished. However, this is not a perfect world. What a designer can do is estimate a time frame based on previous projects. As a designer, I would provide you with a range on every key element in the process--for example, when I estimate the arrival of a piece of furniture, I usually say it could be eight to ten weeks because so many things are out of my control. I can’t control the manufacturing issues or shipping. Delays happen.

I have a saying: “Once something goes south, it does not stop at the border.” That is usually what happens with these projects. Once it starts going sideways, you know you are in for it. "Okay. Let's just have fun because we are going for a ride."

There are so many variables involved in the completion of a project. The best that any designer can do is project a schedule based on similar projects they have completed in the past. Of course, one hiccup can add two weeks onto the project. It is important for clients to be flexible.

For this reason, I suggest that you never plan your design to be completed for a particular holiday or event. There is just no guarantee. Murphy's law will inevitably come into play. If you have a wedding planned for January and it is already October, I cannot promise that the project will be finished by January. I just wouldn't do that to you. And I won't do that to me. It does not mean it can't be done, it just means that, as a designer, I always have to allow for things to come up that were unexpected. The unexpected surprises in every design can alter the schedule. Every situation is different. I can give you a best-case scenario and that is all I can offer. If those planned events are really important I suggest you have a back up plan just in case things don't fall in place, as you would have them.

So if a client is having company at Thanksgiving and asks, "Can you do all of this by then?" My answer is simple, "I will do my best. But there are no guarantees."

There is another alternative that is not as flexible but can work. Instead of customizing the furniture, your designer can purchase the furnishings right off the showroom floor from the design centers. You are still getting beautiful and unique items but you may not have as many choices in colors, fabrics and finishes. You do, however, get everything immediately and there are lots to choose from.

The bottom line: never design a room for a specific occasion. Instead, design the room ahead of time and the occasion will manifest.

How to Get the Best Designer

d randolph foulds photography

Ask the Right Questions

One of the surest ways to know that you have the right designer, one that will be good for you, is to notice if you and your prospective designer can sit down and really communicate with one another. You understand how they view your expectations. You notice that when you are in discussions with your designer, they are really interviewing you--trying to understand you at a deeper level.

Your designer seeks to discover what is it that you truly want. What is it that you really love? What are those things that you don't like? What turns you on? When you share this with your designer, you want to be heard. You want to make sure they get it, that they understand exactly what you are saying. Make sure that they are able to relay your desires back to you in a way that it actually evokes the feeling of: "Ah, they get it. They understand. They are relating to me." That is absolutely critical. It is a vitally important reaction.

You also want a designer with deep experience. Experience is so important. They must have the proficiency and ability to complete the job that you want her to undertake. If it is a job remodeling a kitchen, you do not want this to be the designer's first kitchen. Trust me on this. You do not want that.

One of best ways to hire the right designer is to ask the right questions. Surprisingly, many people ask the wrong questions of their prospective designer. So let's change that. Here are twelve of the most important questions you should ask any prospective designer.

Twelve Questions That You Absolutely Should Ask to Get the Best Designer

(1) What happens if I do not like the design?

This is an excellent question and should be asked early in the process. This question must be answered within whatever contractual relationship you establish with your designer.

First of all, at every step--from the beginning of the project to the end--you should always be involved. So with a good designer, it rarely if ever happens, that at the end of the project a client would say they do not like the design. It has never happened with me. By the time you get to the end of the project, you have been so involved in the process and have made so many decisions, that you would never claim not to like the design. The ideal designer has paid attention to your reactions and listened to what you want. So you will love the design if you are involved in creating it and approving elements throughout the entire process.

So, ask this upfront: "What if I do not like the design?" When you ask me that question, I can then describe the design process. I can explain how you are going to be involved--how you are going to be making decisions and signing off on everything that happens all the way to the end.

A good designer will make sure that everything is extremely clear and that you sign off when there is a problem or opportunity—basically at every milestone. For example, if something unexpected happens, I bring you into the process and provide full disclosure. I present you options and suggestions then move forward in whatever direction you choose. I prefer to get your agreement step by step throughout the whole process. My clients find this to be engaging, exciting, and fun.

All of this should be spelled out in the written agreement between you and your designer. What is the process? What are the steps? When do I need to be involved as a client? All of this needs to be documented and understood.

Everyone is excited in the beginning, so both you and your designer need to be careful not to skip these steps. When I begin a project, I am just as excited as you are, so I always make a point of going over the contract with you.

During the design and implementation process, I refer back to our contractual agreement. As a client, you must understand that agreement. You, too, should refer back to it constantly because things do happen. When things come up, everyone can get excited and you might forget what you signed-off on. Referring back to the contract is important. It ensures the outcome you want.

(2) *Who Buys the Furniture?*

The Unexpected Sofa

I was under contract with a client in the middle of the job. We had just completed the design phase and were setting up the purchasing agreement for the approved furnishings. The whole design had been pulled together. It was absolutely beautiful. It was exactly what they said they wanted. Everything was fitting together nicely into the project: the lighting, rugs, upholstered furniture, case goods, accessories, flooring and window treatments. It was the total package.

I arrive at their home to meet with them to go over the design. When I walked in, I saw a brand new sofa sitting in front of me! This sofa was not even remotely like the one we had selected. I asked, "What is this?" Their response: "I couldn't help myself. I walked into this store and I thought it was so beautiful." Yes, it was beautiful. The problem was that it did not fit in the design scheme that had been tightly pulled together. The fabric, color and scale or size would not work with all the other selections.

In order that my client still has the outcome they wanted I would have to make major adjustments. I had to say, "Now that you have purchased this, I need to go back and pull the whole design together differently based on this piece. Now I am working with something totally different. Can it be done? Absolutely. Is it going to be as beautiful as the first? I do not know, but I can tell you this is going to add more time and money to the whole design process because the entire space had to be re-designed.

It is never good to throw in a new element near the end of the design phase without talking to your designer about your plans. It does happen, though, because people get really excited. They see things they like and decide, "I know this is it." At times, people even purchase things they later hate. But for some reason in the store the salesperson convinced them that this was absolutely the best. Of course, they can't return it and so now we need to start the design process over again. This means another design fee, usually many additional hourly fees. There is a penalty for the decision to buy furniture without communicating first.

Can you buy your own furniture? Does the designer purchase your new furniture? Can we do both? How can you be involved? These are critical and very important questions. Remember there is the separation between the design phase, the purchasing phase, and the construction phase. Each phase has a fee attached to it. Actually you may only want to hire your designer to do the design, the layout, choose the colors, and choose the fabrics. Then they can turn it all over to you to implement those recommendations. You can go into the retail world and purchase the specified products. That is possible.

However, by working with your designer and having them purchase the items on your behalf, sometimes you can get some price advantage over retail stores. You definitely will save lots of time and lessen the chance of making expensive mistakes. As a professional designer, I do not purchase for my clients through retail stores unless they have a special design program that still allows me to work indirectly with the manufacturer. I definitely do not work with the big box retail stores. I deal directly with manufacturers or 'to the trade only' programs. I always try to pass on some advantages, if possible. So, yes, you can purchase on your own. But you are limited, especially if custom items are in the design specifications--because who is going to do the work? You may not have access to those resources, where your designer does. Your decision will depend on what works best for you and your project.

(3) What are your qualifications?

This is an excellent question. Also to what associations do you belong? Raw talent is fine, but you want a trained professional--someone who understands code issues and new technologies. You also want a designer who stays current, who completes their continuing education every year, attends seminars and events in the furniture market, etc. In other words, a professional who is doing everything they can to stay in touch and in step with the latest in their industry.

You want a designer with the requisite educational qualifications and degrees and who is continually learning and growing in the interior design field.

(4) What are you doing to stay current with the latest in technology and advancements in design?

That is a very reasonable question to ask. It is all about continuing education. I am an Allied Member of ASID, which is the largest professional association for interior designers. ASID requires ten CEUs (Continuing Education Units) every two years. Usually two to three times a year, I attend seminars at the big trade shows, design centers and home furnishing market to learn about the recent technologies and trends. Seminars are also available presenting the new requirements and building codes.

I attend the largest European international (trade-only) furnishings market in Paris every few years. I love shopping at this market. It is in one of my favorite cities and they have an out-of-this-world, fabulous flea market for unique finds and vintage pieces. This is another special way I serve my clients. I can even arrange a fabulous international shopping spree trip, to take my clients to these flea markets. All these furnishing markets are critical because manufacturers from all over the world come together in one place to display their latest productions. They are huge, some up to a million industry attendees. It is not open to the public, only to members of the trade. I am able to view the new collections and talk with manufacturers, see how things are made and decide what vendors I want to add to my arsenal.

I care about quality, about where and how things are manufactured, not just about price. If I were hiring a designer, I would definitely want her to be involved in these kinds of activities.

(5) Do you have references or samples of your work?

That is a great question. Every professional designer should be able to show evidence of what they have accomplished. They should have references. Depending on privacy needs or desires, past clients may not want to be contacted but they may have written a letter of reference. Or for certain online sites, they may have sent in a testimonial.

Not only do you want references you also want to see their work. In most instances you will not be able to visit the past clients' homes, but most designers photograph their work after it is completed. You should be able to see the photographs. How else would you know that this person is capable of doing what they say they are going to do?

Look for a history of happy clients served by the interior designer you are considering. You may not be able to actually speak to them, but you definitely want to know that there are satisfied people behind the designer. Look for common threads of satisfaction in the testimonials and reference letters.

(6) Do you have contractors you like to use?

Asking if I have my own contractors is a reasonable question. As a designer, I keep a list of contractors that I can refer. The complexity of the job determines what contractor I prefer to work with. In fairness to all the contractors, I usually give the client two or three names of contractors they can interview. Normally I prefer that my clients contract them directly. It saves them money. It also makes the job a little less complicated.

I am choosy myself, so if you have a contractor that you want me to work with, I am perfectly willing to do so, as long as they are licensed and have the requisite experience. I need to see a portfolio or testimonials from some of the projects or designers that they have worked with in the past.

(7) How do you interpret my vision?

This is a great question to ask your interior designer. In the first hour or so with your designer, you share a lot of information. You ask and answer many questions like: What are your favorite colors? What are the things that inspire you? What do you do...? How do you do this…? The purpose is to get you to reveal your vision.

The pragmatic questions are easy. As your designer, I want to make sure we are on the same page.

And you want this too. The best way to find out is to ask your designer, "What do you think about what I have asked you to do for me? How do you envision my project?" This is important and they will tell you. It does not take a designer long to formulate that vision.

As designers, we are imagining from the moment we walk through the door. We are visual people and we make very quick assessments based on how you live, on how you dress, and on the things that are around you. All of that is done in a matter of minutes. After interviewing my clients, it is not difficult for me to tell them what I think is their vision. That is key. That doesn't mean I can or will tell them how I would design their space. It does mean I can discuss the goals and the overall feeling of the spaces.

(8) How can you help me if I really don't know what I want?

It is not unusual for a person not to fully know what they want and, at the same time, know that they need my help.

As a professional, I am not asking my clients to give me a road map to a particular design. I want to know: How do you live? What makes you happy? With what do you surround yourself? What is your most comfortable chair and why is that chair so comfortable? Why do you like certain things? I really get into the heart of what makes my client tick.

You want a designer who is able to use that information to design spaces and select elements that will support all those wonderful things that you say you love.

There are a few things that your designer will do to help you. One, guide you through the whole process from beginning to end. You will know what to expect.

You can expect to see drawings or storyboards. I use 3-D Design or digital design boards for representation of how the final space will look. Your designer should let you see and touch the fabric samples and provide you with a floor and furniture plan.

My goal in this phase is to use all of the tools accessible to me so that you can literally, not just envision the design in your mind, but you can actually see it, whether it is digital, a hard copy drawing, or on a design story board. Storyboards are great because you will see all of the elements in front of you showing the vibrancy and all of the different colors and textures. All the things we talked about in our initial conversations that make you smile.

The design process itself becomes an experience of self-discovery.

(9) What designs have you done to address needs similar to my project?

Another great question! You want to know if this designer is the right designer for your job. One of the ways to determine this is to ask if they have completed this type of design work before. Have they overcome the same challenges in the past that you are presenting to them now? Can they do this? There are several ways that you can tell. One is to look at their portfolio. The other is to examine their references because you might be asking your designer to do something totally different. Perhaps they may not have experience with this type of project, but based on their skill level, experience, client testimonials, education, and expertise, you can transfer all of that over to, "Oh, without a doubt, they could do this."

That being said no two projects are alike. You want to know if this designer is capable. In the end, this is a judgment call on your part. You also want to have some indication of your designer's temperament. Will you enjoy working with them? Does your designer make you feel happy? Does your designer make you feel warm? Do they appear to understand? Are they listening to you? Does your designer's temperament align with yours? It is not a question you ask, but it is definitely a noticing that you pay attention to when you are interviewing a designer.

(10) What do you offer that is different from all the other designers?

This an excellent question to ask a designer during their interview. What sets you apart? Listen carefully. Try to see how this designer is unique. They may talk about their experience: how long have they been doing this work and how many clients have been satisfied. They might give you some examples, but there are other things to consider.

As designers we all believe we are different. That is because we are different! From the start our perspective differs.

As you interview a prospective designer you will want to know how they are different. Why are they special enough to be hired? This is when you should start paying attention to the confidence your designer is projecting. You will need a designer that is extremely confident.

Life experience and knowledge beyond interior design comes into play. For example, my clients definitely have an advantage in that I am an architect by trade. Architecture adds another deeper aspect of knowledge to interior design.

If you asked me the question "What makes you different?", here is how I would respond: "It is more than my education (the Masters I have in architecture, which makes me an architect by trade). Consider the twenty-nine years of my life where I traveled all over the world. This created in me an expansive mindset when it comes to culture, architecture and design."

Perhaps that is one reason why I strive to have a 100% client satisfaction, and so far so good. I have not had a client come back to me and say, "I do not like this." I have only had them say, "Oh my God! This has changed my life." What really makes me different? I pride myself on listening to you and getting into your heart. I love really understanding YOU. I do not judge. My goal is to help you get to where you want to go. That is the way I am."

(11) Are there any cost saving measures we can use without compromising the design?

No matter what price point you set, budget is one of life's realities. Whether you are at a low, medium, or highest level price point, the design is always about budget, budget, and budget. At every level you always wish you had a little more than you planned.

"How can I have it all?" is a good question to ask your designer. A great designer will creatively navigate you through all the different issues that show up and find solutions that you can't even dream of. Can you achieve the overall vision? Can you still get the "Wow!" factor if you include some cost saving measures in the design? Can we delay some items if their absence would not compromise the design? Ask your designer because there are always ways to do that. Always.

(12) What should I expect in and during the design process and what is the timeline?

Hopefully, before you even ask this question, the designer will have gone over what to expect. Once you have an idea of the nature and scope of the project, your designer should set expectations. When I sit down with my clients, I say,

"Okay, this is how we are going to do this." We are in a contract together--that is not just a legal term, it means that you (the client) and I (the designer) are working on this together.

We establish rules on how we work together. Some of these are included in the legal agreement, but we also need an understanding. You need to know what to expect. The worst thing that could happen in a project is a step being overlooked. Not knowing what to expect can cause a lot of anxiety. If an unforeseen situation comes out of the blue, it is not a comfortable position for the designer either. It is really important for the designer to let the client know that when the unexpected shows up there is a protocol in place to resolve the issue.

48 Days to a Place You Love… Step by Step

d randolph foulds photography

STEP 1: Take a Look Around

Begin by noticing. Enter through your front door just like you are a visitor for the first time. Walk through every room and notice what you see and how you feel in the space. Is the space inspiring? Is the room dated from 1950? Is this an important space? Is this a new space that you haven't seen in two months because you never go in there? Ask yourself: what makes you feel good? What makes you smile? What is important to you? What will elevate you in this space, in your space? What room is the most important to you personally? Notice what is going on in your house. You have to look around and take it in. That is where to begin.

If you conclude that you really need to invest in your entire home, sit down and think about which room would be the most fulfilling to have done first? If you entertain a lot, this might end up being one of the more public spaces in the home: the living room, the dining room, or maybe, the family room. To you, the entertainer, these may seem to be the more important spaces.

Sometimes, the place to begin is the master bedroom. For some reason, the bedroom is often the last room to be designed. That should not hold true, as a rule, but more often than not it is. The bedroom is the most personal, private and intimate space in your home. It should always be just about you. It should be a very special place in your home because it is a reflection of how you feel about yourself. This says a lot. I have been told that it is the least important room because nobody sees it. WOW. The most important person in the world sees it--YOU. You might look around and see that you basically are sleeping on the floor with mattresses, or you have your parents' leftover furniture that you have been carrying around for the last 25 years. Even worse, it is your first bedroom 'set' from your first apartment (20 years ago).

We tend to shortchange ourselves--not giving ourselves the luxury of a fabulous bedroom that reflects and protects the deepest parts of us. So maybe you want to start there, so that you can enjoy all the love you can give yourself. This is usually the first and last room you see everyday. Focus in on what you need and what would make the biggest impact in your life. It just might be the master bedroom.

Consider construction. You may need some professional help in deciding how the project should unfold because construction can be disruptive. It is not just isolated to one room; it usually affects other spaces. This domino effect should to be taken into account.

Take the pressure off of yourself. If you really want to redesign your master bedroom, but you do often entertain and feel that needs to be done first, be kind to yourself. Don't judge. It will take you further and give you the energy to do more. You can always swing back around and do the other spaces. This is how you start prioritizing what you are going to do first. Ask your designer. They definitely will help you with that, but I would want you to have some ideas beforehand.

You might want to consider your time schedule. If we are in September and you know that you have big family events for the holidays, do not start construction. As a matter of fact, do not start the project. You need to start your project early in the summer if you are going to have holiday guests and parties. The more time you have, the more likely everything will be ready and the less stress you will feel.

Also consider your finances. How are you going to pay for this? Are you using your credit cards? A home loan? Your reserve? Resolve these questions because they definitely affect your project. You might say this seems pretty basic and common sense. But I cannot tell you how many times I discovered the financial commitment had not been fully planned and in place before the project began. This is another reason I make sure we have a real sit down at the initial consultation. I like to talk about money early. To some it is uncomfortable and maybe insulting. But in all these "dream come true ideas" and creativity, there are some real world opportunities and it takes money. I also suggest that there is contingency money stashed away for the just-in-case expenses outside the budget.

I notice that a money block comes in different forms. The most usual is that in the middle of the project after everything has been designed, selected, and ready to order, I start to get a lot of push back. Sometimes I am confused, thinking that maybe I missed the mark on recommendations. But in digging a little harder I realize the desire is strong, but the money is not there. Honesty about money is critical in working with your designer!

Before contacting a designer you might want to consider looking through your favorite design magazines to get inspiration. Just see what is out there. What are other people doing? What is the new thing that attracts you? What are some of the elements that you like or dislike--the things that you see when you open up a page and you say, "Oh my God. I could never do this." This is great information for your designer: "I saw this in a magazine and it was hideous." With this information, your designer can get into why you experienced that reaction. The whys are so important for discerning who you are, what you need, and what you want.

It also does something else. It puts you in the mood. It gets you excited about the possibility of having a fabulous space--maybe one that is going to be featured in a magazine. All of this prepares you for what is yet to come. Go online and look at designs, including mine. Start putting together a folder of your favorites. Or better yet, put together a vision board of what your best self can dream!

When you are looking at a designer's profile always read what people have to say about the designs. Read client testimonials, especially the ones that are specific and include good information--that tell you why they love or like the designer.

For a designer, the process of gathering independent testimonials can be frightening (especially on some online and social media sites) because we have no idea what our clients are going to say. Some organizations contact my clients and ask them to write a testimonial. Then it goes public. I see it at the same time that everybody else sees it. It is always a joy when I read one that tells others what I did or explains why the design was special to them, or why they would hire me again.

You need to hear these testimonials as well. Then you can make the call and set up an appointment.

STEP 2: Vision - Begin With the End in Mind

Before you even make your first phone call to a designer, just sit with yourself for a minute and really think about what is it that you want done. Not the particulars--leave that to the professional. What vision do you want to share with the designer? How do you really want to feel in your space? These are things that you need to consider before you talk with your first designer.

Don't worry early in the process about price and bargaining. Instead, focus on the end result: what will make you happy?

Neither you nor your future designer wants this to be an arduous process. You want it to be fun. You want to be energized and excited. So, do your homework. Figure out what you want. The designer, if they are trained well, will take what you share and show you how you can achieve your goals. But first you need to know where you want to go.

You may say, "What if I don't know what I want?" I say everyone knows what they love and what they really want to experience. We are back to the judgment and shame I mentioned earlier, that so many women in charge take on. Dreaming about what you love is freeing without any pressure. Give yourself permission to just enjoy what that feels like. STOP judging and just dream!

STEP 3: A Realistic Budget

The next question in the real world is this: what is my budget? Not "what do things cost?" because as a professional, I do not expect you to know what things cost. But you must know how much money you are willing to invest in your mind's vision. How important is that vision to you? How much money is available to you? You need to know and understand that before engaging a designer.

Because most people have only been through construction once, or maybe never, they really do not have any idea of what things cost. Even with furniture, people still have no idea what things cost. You putting a budget together can be difficult. Your designer is going to help you with that. So if you are looking at a sofa that you just love and the sofa costs $9000, you have a choice, "I can buy that," or "No, I want that look but $9000 is not what I want to spend on a sofa."

It's similar to the question: which came first the chicken or the egg? Sometimes, you need your designer to come in and give you an idea. This is why I always advise my clients to do a paid consultation with me first because we need to talk budget. I make sure you have an idea of what a budget should include. When I help create a budget for you, I offer many possibilities or options in: good, better and best categories.

Keep in mind that all the products will be of good quality. The difference will be in the details. The "good" design is simpler, probably using less designer brand named elements. The "better" design is a mix of a few "best" elements and some of the "good". For the "best", you get top of the line custom designed high-end fabrics, trims, and furniture. This might include name brands and designer brands in the mix. Your designer should be able to estimate a room at all levels. For example, this room at a good level is estimated to be about $15,000, in the better category about

$22,000 to $25,000 and for the best, the cost will start at about $30,000."

Now, for some people these numbers are fine. For others the response may be, "Oh, no. I can't do this. That is too much at this time." In this situation you have choices. Maybe you only want to purchase the design portion and then do all the work yourself. For example, I offer a program called Your Design Toolbox where I create the overall room design, floor plan, furniture plan and color palette. I also select the flooring, lighting and accessories for you based on your budget and a completed detailed questionnaire about your vision, goals and preferences. You then purchase all the furnishings on your own time schedule as well as implement the painting, wall covering or suggested design elements. With the package you receive complete easy to follow instructions to begin and finish your project (step one, step two, step three, etc.) and get the end result you want. All product suggestions (furniture, lighting, flooring, accessories, etc.) you can buy directly using online retailers. This program is a great option for those who really like to get in the mix and enjoy doing the work themselves. Or maybe they want an overall master plan and the ability to carry it out over a longer period of time. Also, this has been a great option for some of my clients who are abroad or in other states that really love my designs. Not every designer offers this type of service.

STEP 4: Choose Your Ideal Designer

Now you are ready to contact and interview designers. Get references from friends, especially if you have seen the designer's work in your friend's home and like what you see. You can call ASID to find qualified designers in your area. You can visit sites like houzz.com. Online tools are available for you to view the work of many designers and make an assessment. Who is this person? How is their website or portfolio? Do they have a video? Do your due diligence.

Some people want to interview one or two designers. Others come straight out and say, "Okay, I am going to interview one and see how it works out. I like this designer so far on paper and I love the videos. I like their personality. This designer seems to know what they are doing."

You have already identified much of what you want to do and how much you are willing to invest, so now it is time to call and set up an appointment.

Do not set out to interview ten designers. That is the worst thing that you could do--it just gets to be too confusing. It becomes a job and that is not what you want.

Instead, after you do your homework well, pick one or two and call them. (Of course you could just go to my website and find that you are so in love with what you see, you just call me!) OK that was my shameful plug. Seriously, I would recommend interviewing three at the most. That is it!

Your Ideal Designer?

You need a good relationship with your designer. They need to be someone who really listens to you and understands you. This doesn't mean that you and your designer are always going to agree. Your designer is a professional and is obligated to share the facts with you.

As a professional, I know what I know. When I give clients information that I have researched, it is well thought out and it is factual. This does not mean it is always the end-all but it does mean that it is not just a guess. You want a relationship where your designer can say, "That is just not going to work. I don't care how much you love it, it is not going to work." Then, they can tell you why it is not going to work and offer some alternatives to give you the concept you desire.

You have to be open to that. Some people do not like to be told "no". In situations where I deal with powerful female CEOs, I find they are not used to having somebody say, "No. That is not going to work." Or "I cannot recommend this." If you engage a designer, they are there to make sure that the project is done correctly. You have to give her the room to do it. You both must be very honest with each other in the relationship.

You will also need to be vulnerable. Private information is disclosed, especially financial information. As a designer, at times I feel more like a nurse or a psychologist or even a teacher. All this is under the umbrella of interior designer. I see many personal things in people's homes, so the relationship must be based on trust.

When your designer says they are going to do something, then they should do it. If something comes up where they can't, they should be able to say, "I am sorry. I apologize for this not happening and this is how I am going to rectify it. This is how we can make this work." You are building a friendship based on trust, honesty, and sincerity, including being open to say, "This is not right. It is not going to work."

Intimacy

At times, I experience clients who are guarded at first, especially couples. One person may not want the other one to know what is going on and I, unfortunately, find myself in the position of knowing both sides. In this, I must balance what I can and cannot reveal. If you have marital problems, your designer might become a "marriage counselor"--hearing both sides.

I try to remove myself from these situations as much as possible. At the same time I must get things done and so I need to ask certain questions. Sometimes, marital problems are revealed with the design itself because there wasn't necessarily an agreement ahead of time on how much money would be spent.

Once, I designed two rooms for a client at a cost of about $88,000. She never blinked an eye. The space was spectacular. Unfortunately, she had never really discussed the actual amount with her husband. When he saw the final invoice, paid in full, he erupted: "You spent $88,000!" I sat there trying to melt into the chair as they went at it. Keep in mind; this is a multi-million dollar house. The home and the design are upscale. However, his value system was under attack. He could not understand why "furniture, window treatments, and a couple of pillows" would cost $88,000. The house was huge, 9000 square feet, but this did not matter. In a situation like this, I have actually excused myself and left.

As a designer, I now insist that anybody who is signing the check or financially responsible must be involved in the process. This is non-negotiable. No one wants these kinds of surprises otherwise this may happen. When the project is finished I need to know that I am not going to witness a major argument. That would be so uncomfortable.

I remember a time when my client's wife did not know that her husband had brought in an interior designer. He did not tell her. He told me she was out of town and "when she gets back, she is looking forward to working with me". This was a construction project. When she returned home, several walls in the house had been taken down. She was not happy.

These are invaluable experiences. Now, I insist that all decision makers are on board. I no longer assume that couples had their conversation about money and these conflicts are usually about money.

The net is this: your designer will see everything. Your designer will see if your household is unified or not. They will see how separated you are. They witness arguments obviously. As clients, you are exposed, as are your finances.

A Gift for You

For your complimentary *Design•ology Checklist:*

How to Hire a Designer That Will Work For YOU, visit

www.designologybook.com

Ready to Begin?

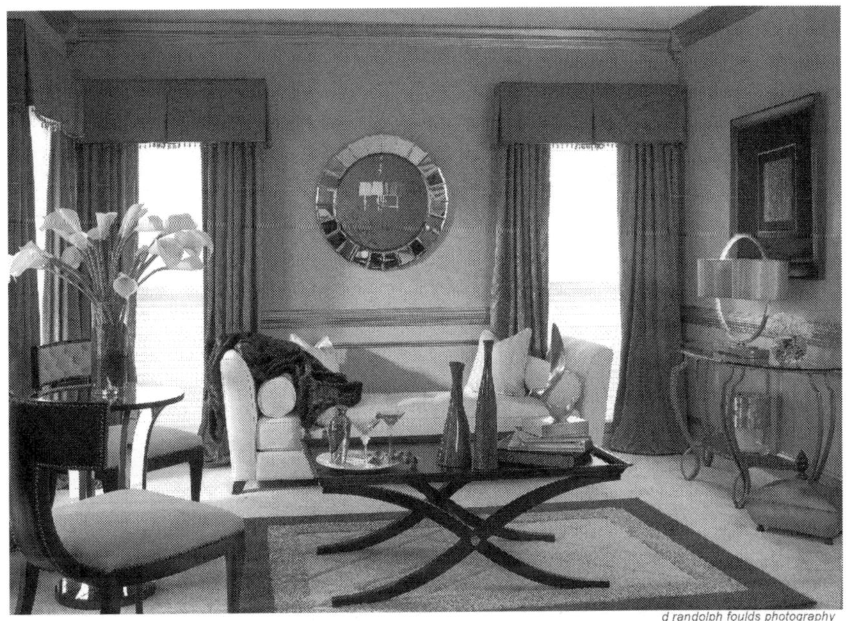

d randolph foulds photography

Consider a Designer

If you are a female, powerful CEO at the top of your game, yet when you come home, it is just not all that it is supposed to be, then a designer can help you. Your home needs to represent and support you. If you feel that something is missing, your home does not delight you, then consider hiring a designer.

As women we are all precious cargo. We really are. We are beautiful vessels and we should surround ourselves with beauty inside and out. You deserve a beautiful home. You deserve to celebrate all that you have accomplished--every single day--but in a way that is authentic to who you are. You want a place you and your family can call home--one that reflects you. You need a designer that can help you on that journey.

Am I the Interior Designer for You?

What you see is what you get with me. I do not hide. I never said that I was a designer for everyone. I am not. But for my ideal client, I am definitely the best designer that they will ever find because I hone in on exactly what they need.

Why? Because I have lived a full life! I really have. I have done so much in my life and have had many successes. I enjoy doing the things that I do. People trust my experience as a designer. They see it and they trust it. I have a Master's degree in architecture--something I do not throw out there lightly because getting that degree was probably one of the hardest challenges of my life.

It was very difficult. At that time there were very few Black women with Master of Architectural degrees in this country. So many obstacles were put in front of me. I am proud that I overcame those obstacles and did well. Now, I carry a certain confidence and my clients appreciate that. They notice that I am comfortable with all aspects of designing their home.

I know what I am doing

For a very long time, I travelled. I have been to every continent at least five or six times. And with that comes a genuine curiosity and an appreciation for different cultures. I tap into that energy to help me understand even more the person that I am there to serve.

The bottom line: if you are open, then I can help you identify what is missing in your home and pull all your desires together. If this sounds interesting to you, be sure to visit me at http://www.decoriadesigns.com.

You Deserve a Home That Supports You

You deserve a space that is inviting, one that is joyful and comfortable, one that is an authentic reflection of who you are and also of where you are in life. I should not walk into a female CEO's, or any CEO's, home office and find milk crates holding up books. If you are doing this, it is probably not because you like milk crates. It is because you have not taken the time to find a beautiful piece of furniture that you love and that will hold the books that you love.

It is time to honor yourself. That is what I want your home to do--to honor you. I want it to honor your family. You cannot do that with milk crates. I want you, the CEO who has stepped up in every other area of her life, to step up into this one.

Step up because that is one way to put closure to all of the "I am not good enough" stuff that goes along with the workplace competitiveness, or the "I always have to be the best". You do not have to engage in any of that negative talk. You just have to be in your space and love it and love you in your space. That is what I want for you.

One of the ways to do this is to hire a professional. You do not have the time to learn design on top of everything else you have to do. You do have time to look at magazines. You have time to play. You have time to have fun. But you do not have time to pull a design together and do the work that it requires. Let the professional be an expert at what you are looking for and help bring you to where you desire to go. You deserve it.

About the Author

Award-winning designer and Décoria Interior Designs founder Sheryl McLean is committed to creating a place that makes you smile each and every time you enter your space. Sheryl's executive clients often say, "This has changed my life!"

It's not just that Sheryl is a UCLA-trained architect and international design expert or that for nearly thirty years she traveled the world with an eye on culture, architecture and design elements. It's because Sheryl is the kind of woman who knows what's in your closet and will never tell, who listens to your heart, without judgment. She helps you create a space that reflects who you are, where you are and where you are going in life... a place that nurtures you so that you feel rejuvenated, refreshed and restored. Her work has been featured in design and decorating books and trade magazines internationally.

She is an Allied member of the American Society of Interior Designers (ASID) the most prestigious organization of Interior Design professionals, a certified color specialist and a home automation expert. For more visit: www.decoriadesigns.com

Products By Sheryl McLean

Start your own DIY design project with a professionally designed plan by Décoria Interior Designs: *Your Design Toolbox*

What is Your Design Toolbox?

Imagine a space where you love to just be, where you feel rejuvenated, refreshed, and restored. Award-winning designer and Décoria Interior Designs Founder Sheryl McLean creates a stunningly beautiful and luxurious design for those who want to roll up their sleeves and get to work on their own project.

Your Design Toolbox is a room design for a flat fee. The recommended design elements are based on your budget. A professional designer interviews you and designs your space in 6-8 weeks, where all the fabrics and materials are specified for you. You receive a beautiful box in the mail with drawings, samples, retail and online purchase specifications and detailed instructions for implementing your project. Visit decoriadesigns.com for more information.

Hire Sheryl McLean To Speak at Your Event!

Book Sheryl McLean as your Keynote Speaker and Make Your Event Highly Entertaining and Unforgettable!

For over two decades, Sheryl McLean has been educating, entertaining and helping executives create stunningly beautiful and luxurious spaces that support their life mission.

Her origin story includes her childhood struggles that did not include the finer things in life to later becoming the first African American woman to graduate with a Master's from the UCLA School of Architecture, and building her talents into a successful design company. She shares stories of traveling and studying design trends around the world and the common conflicts the design process evokes at home. Sheryl shares secrets that only an interior designer would know as well as relevant, actionable strategies that anyone can use to create a home that supports them - even if they've never engaged in interior design before.

Her unique style inspires, empowers and entertains audiences while giving them the tools and strategies they need and want to "wake up in their own home."

For More

For more information, visit www.decoriadesigns.com or call +1 (301) 430-0723.

A Gift for You

For your complimentary *Design•ology Checklist:*

How to Hire a Designer That Will Work For YOU, visit

www.designologybook.com

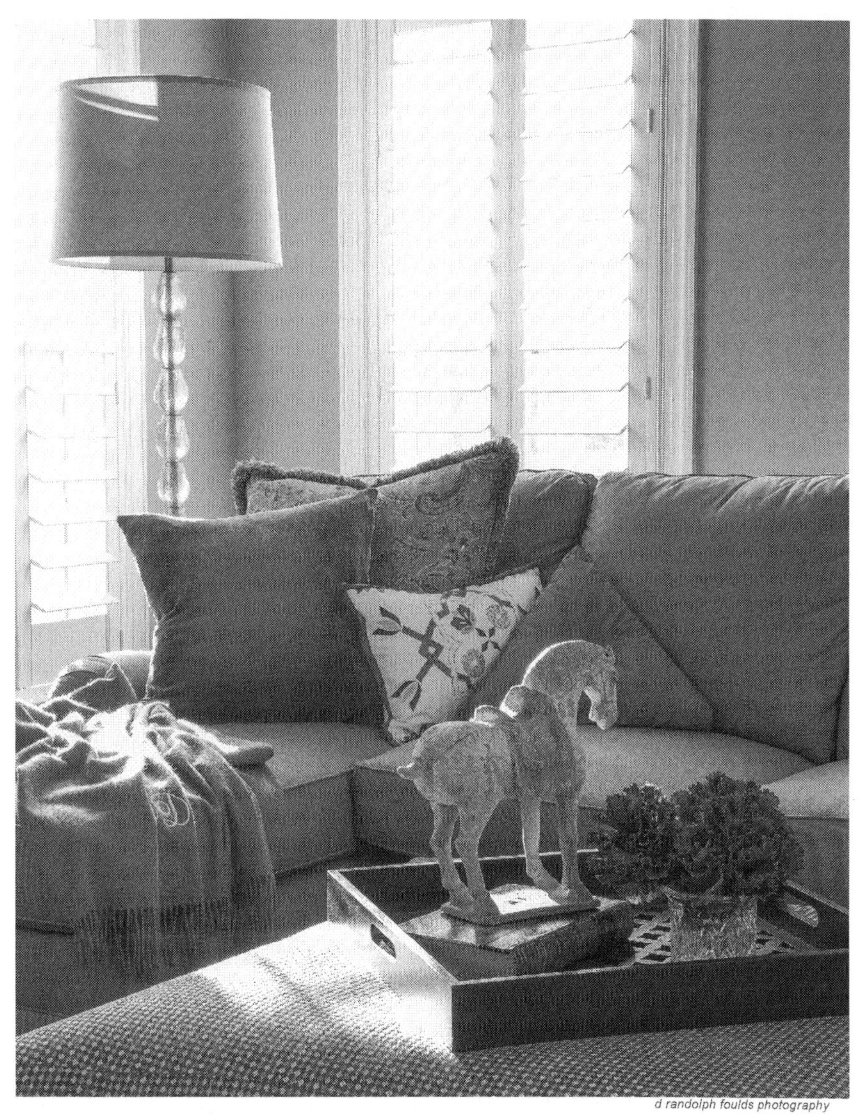

d randolph foulds photography

One Last Thing...

If you enjoyed this book or found it useful I'd be very grateful if you'd post a short review on Amazon. Your support really does make a difference and I read all the reviews personally so I can get your feedback and make this book even better.

If you'd like to leave a review then all you need to do is click the review link on this book's page on Amazon.com.

Thank you for your support!

Sheryl McLean, CEO, Décoria Interior Designs

Made in the USA
Middletown, DE
11 May 2022

65624550R00073